# Homeschooling in New York City

New York was a bustling city after the Civil War. New York City native Theodore Roosevelt Sr. and his wife Martha from Georgia lived there in a grand townhouse. The couple had married in 1853, eight years before the war began. Their five-level home had been a wedding present from Theodore's father. Here Theodore and Martha (known as Mittie) homeschooled their four children: Anna, Theodore Jr., Elliott, and Corinne.

The couple's older son, Theodore Jr., would become the honest, compassionate, hard-working, athletic, enthusiastic, bigger-than-life President Theodore Roosevelt, whose likeness was carved on Mount Rushmore along with George Washington, Thomas Jefferson, and Abraham Lincoln. How did that happen?

**Theodore Roosevelt Jr. at Age 2 in 1861**

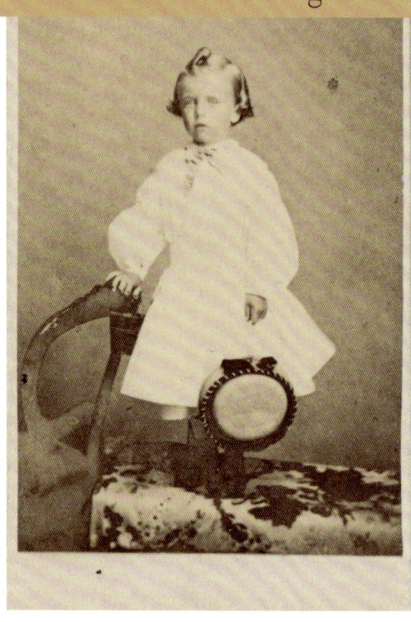

    The Roosevelts made a conscious decision to train their children at home. They believed that attending public school would coarsen—that's the word they used—their children.

    The Roosevelts used tutors as part of their children's education. When the children were young, their tutor was their Aunt Anna, Mittie's sister. Anna had come to live with the Roosevelt family in 1857, the year before Theodore Jr. was born, as did Mittie's mother, whom the children called Grandmamma.

    Of his Aunt Anna, Theodore Jr. later said, "She was as devoted to us children as was my mother herself, and we were equally devoted to her in return." Grandmamma and the children also had a close and affectionate relationship.

Theodore Jr. called her "one of the dearest of old ladies" and said she was "overindulgent" to the children and quite unable to "harden her heart" towards them.

Theodore Roosevelt Sr. took his family responsibilities seriously. Even though Anna was their tutor, Theodore Roosevelt Sr. was the one in charge of his children's education, giving them educational opportunities far beyond the tutoring of Aunt Anna. Theodore Roosevelt Sr. once sent his two boys to study with his own childhood tutor, who lived near their home; but that only lasted a few weeks before the boys came back home to learn.

Until Theodore Roosevelt Jr. entered Harvard University shortly before his 18th birthday, he spent almost all of his time with his family. His playmates and friends were his siblings, his cousins, and the children of his parents' friends. As it turned out, this was wonderful socialization for a future president.

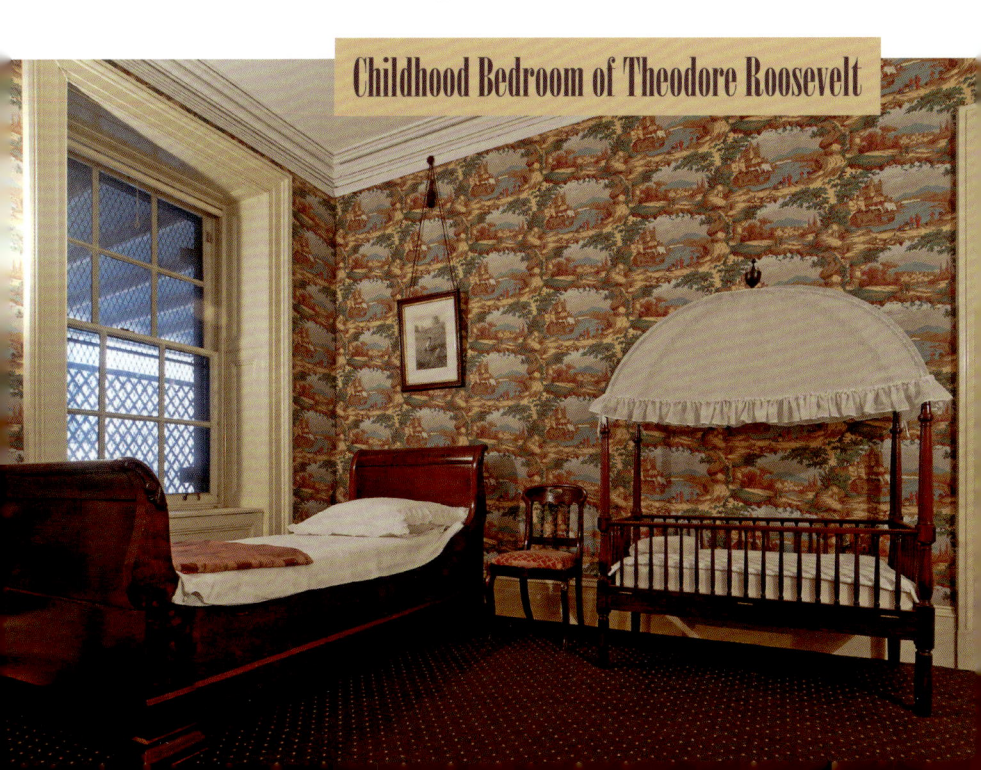

**Childhood Bedroom of Theodore Roosevelt**

Theodore Roosevelt Jr. grew up with the kind of family life that he would one day provide for his own children. In the president's autobiography he wrote about the virtues necessary for a nation:

> [T]hese virtues are as dust on a windy street unless back of them lie the strong and tender virtues of a family life based on the love of the one man for the one woman and on their joyous and fearless acceptance of their common obligation to the children that are theirs.

President Roosevelt understood the value of that kind of marriage and parenting firsthand, since that was exactly the way he had grown up.

Master Bedroom in the Roosevelt Home

# A Strong Marriage

Theodore Sr. was an aristocratic New Yorker. His Roosevelt ancestors immigrated to America from the Netherlands before the American Revolution. Theodore Sr.'s children were the seventh generation of Roosevelts to be born on Manhattan Island. Mittie, on the other hand, was a Southern belle from Roswell, Georgia.

The Civil War began when Theodore Roosevelt Jr. was two and a half years old. His father actively supported the Union, even traveling to Washington, D.C., to do so. While Mr. Roosevelt was a charter member of a club founded to promote the northern cause, Mrs. Roosevelt was sympathetic to the southern cause and had brothers working for it, one as a diplomat in England, another as a blockade runner. Joining Mittie in Confederate sympathies were her mother and her sister Anna.

One night when the children gathered to pray with their mother, young Theodore remembered an incident earlier that day when he believed his mother had been wrong in her maternal discipline. He decided to get back at his mother by praying loudly for the Union army to be successful. He later said that his mother was "not only a most devoted mother, but was also blessed with a strong sense of humor." His prayer made her too tickled to punish him.

When Theodore Roosevelt Sr. traveled away from home on occasion during the war, his mother-in-law, his sister-in-law, and his wife took the opportunity to pack shirts, socks, and toiletries to send to family and friends inside the Confederacy.

**Theodore and Mittie Roosevelt**

President Theodore Roosevelt's parents lived with one another and loved one another through the war even with strongly different beliefs. When Theodore Roosevelt became President of the United States, he helped to negotiate peace between Russia and Japan during the Russo-Japanese War and won the Nobel Peace Prize for doing so. Perhaps he learned something about making peace between two opposing sides in his own boyhood home.

*Photo at right: Parlor in the Roosevelt Home*

# Heart, Soul, Mind, and Body

## Character and Curiosity

The Roosevelt children were nourished by the love of their family and by the Christian teachings of their father. Theodore Roosevelt Sr. was remembered for his affectionate nature. His nephew Emlen described him as "a large, broad, bright, cheerful man with an intense sympathy with everything you brought to him. He loved children especially."

### Library in the Roosevelt Home

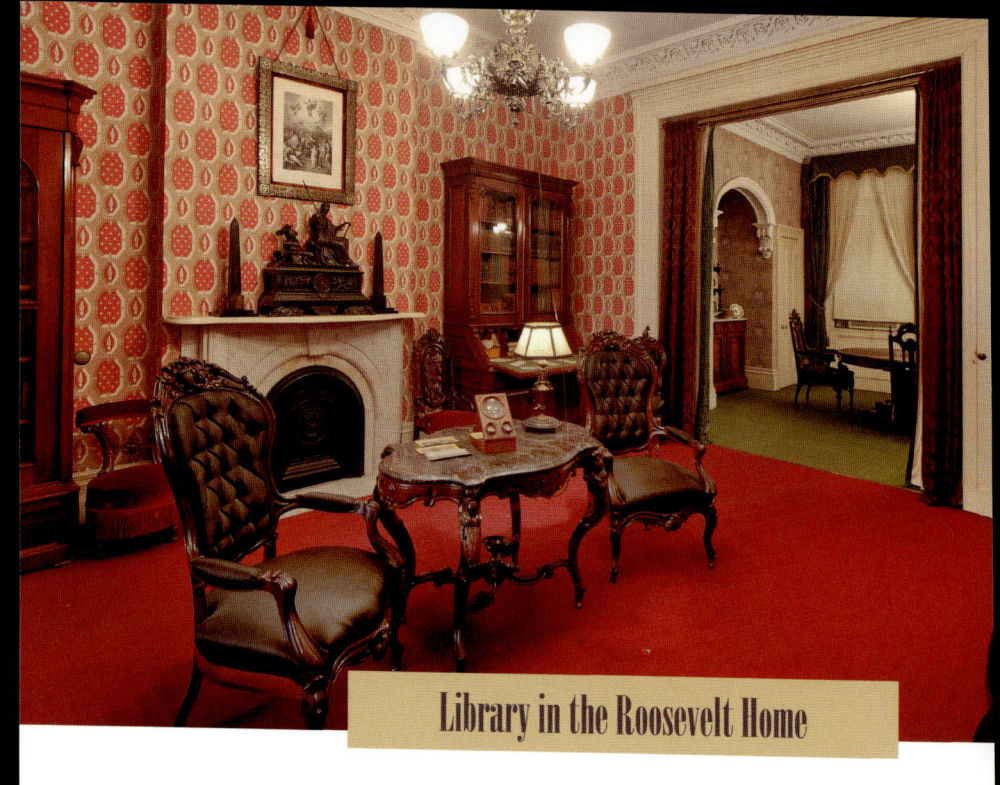

Theodore Roosevelt Sr. himself once wrote to his older daughter, "I always believe in showing affection by doing what will please the one we love, not by talking." Theodore Sr. loved his own mother. He and his four brothers visited her every day. Theodore Jr. would later describe her as "a woman of singular sweetness and strength."

The Roosevelt family enjoyed nicknames. Though politicians later called President Theodore Roosevelt "Teddy," his family called him "Teedie." The Roosevelt children adored their mother Mittie, whom young Teedie and his siblings called Little Motherling. In his autobiography, Teedie described her as "a sweet, gracious, beautiful Southern woman, a delightful companion and beloved by everybody."

The Roosevelts provided Teedie and his siblings with an encouraging atmosphere. They were lifestyle learners.

They learned in the great outdoors. The children read extensively, and their father read aloud to them. The Roosevelts did not allow their children to read the cheap, unwholesome novels that were popular in the day, but good books were plentiful. President Roosevelt later said:

> I think there ought to be children's books. I think that the child will like grown-up books also, and I do not believe a child's book is really good unless grown-ups get something out of it.

Theodore Roosevelt Jr. at Age 7 in 1865

The Roosevelts also subscribed to a children's magazine called *Our Young Folks*. President Roosevelt and his wife shared with their own children the copies of this magazine they saved from their childhoods. Roosevelt said that they were "first-class, good healthy stories, interesting in the first place, and in the next place teaching manliness, decency, and good conduct."

Teedie also enjoyed "girls' stories" such as *Little Women*, *Little Men*, and *An Old Fashioned Girl* by Louisa May Alcott. His reading of Longfellow's poem, "The Saga of King Olaf" gave him a lifelong interest in Scandinavian literature. Because of his interest in science, Teedie remembered disliking *Swiss Family Robinson* because of "the wholly impossible collection of animals met by that worthy family as they ambled inland from the wreck."

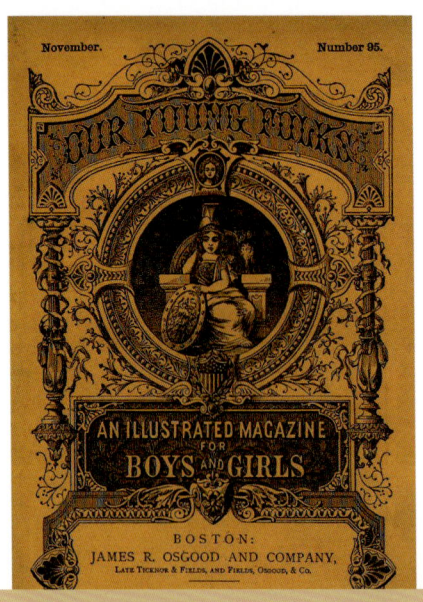

November 1872 Issue of *Our Young Folks*

**Bulloch Hall, Mittie Roosevelt's Childhood Home, in Roswell, Georgia**

    Theodore and Mittie encouraged their children to ask questions of their parents and other adults. The Roosevelts showed hospitality graciously and frequently, so there were plenty of adults around.

    Mittie, Aunt Anna, and Grandmamma nourished the children's imaginations with many stories about life in the South. Mittie and Anna told tales about Daniel Boone and Davy Crockett, and about hunting fox, deer, and wildcat. The stories were so vivid that when Teedie finally got to visit his mother's home after becoming president, he felt "as if I already knew every nook and corner of it."

The Roosevelt children enjoyed the visits their Uncle Hilborne made each summer. He told them great stories, too. He also read Shakespeare and performed the plays for the children.

The senior Roosevelt gave his children his undivided attention. His younger son Elliott once said that his father was "one of those rare grown men who seem never to forget that they were once children themselves."

Theodore Roosevelt Sr. taught his children's hearts. He paid close attention to their character and taught them to cultivate a hopeful disposition. As an adult, President Roosevelt wrote this about his father:

> **My father, Theodore Roosevelt, was the best man I ever knew. He combined strength and courage with gentleness, tenderness, and great unselfishness. He would not tolerate in us children selfishness or cruelty, idleness, cowardice, or untruthfulness.**

Theodore Roosevelt Sr. taught the children to be busy and to enjoy being busy. He was an example of the active, joyful life he encouraged in his children. He and Mittie loved going to parties, where he was known to dance all night. Theodore Sr. also had a great fondness for horses, which he rode in New York's Central Park.

**1869 Drawing of Central Park**

Theodore Jr. later wrote:

**I never knew anyone who got greater joy out of living than did my father or anyone who more whole-heartedly performed every duty; and no one whom I have ever met approached his combination of enjoyment of life and performance of duty.**

Anyone who has studied President Roosevelt will recognize immediately that he took to heart his father's instruction to enjoy life and be busy. Teedie's older sister Anna, whom the family called "Bamie," said, "There was never anyone so wonderful as my father."

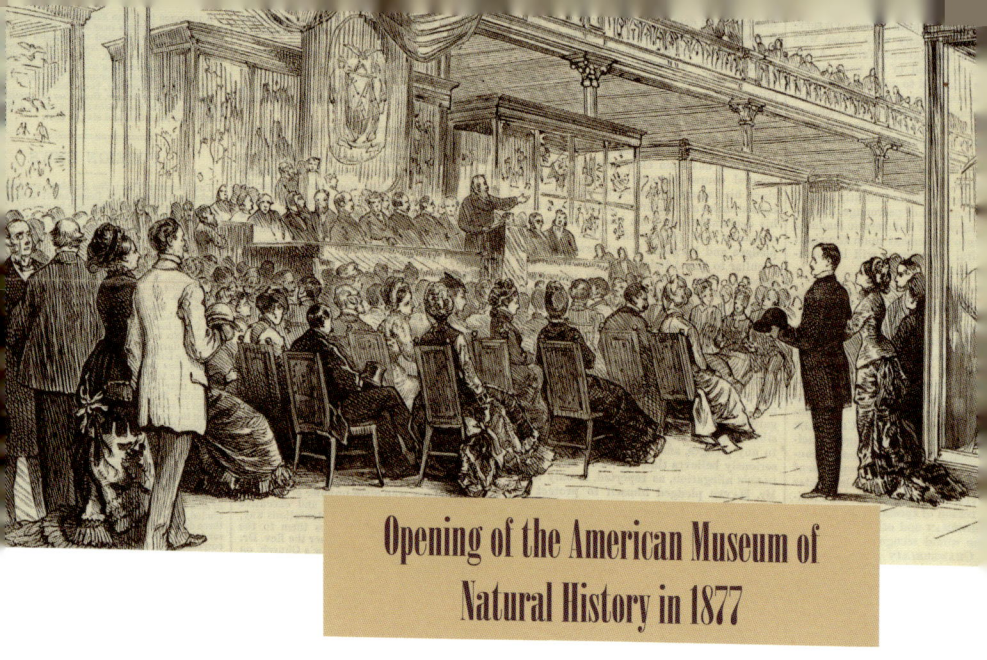

*Opening of the American Museum of Natural History in 1877*

## Loving God and Loving Neighbors

  Theodore Roosevelt Sr. taught his own children about God. Each morning Theodore Jr. would wait at the bottom of the stairs with his younger brother and sister to accompany their father to the library where they would pile on the sofa with him for morning prayers. In Theodore Jr.'s boyhood journal, he wrote of a time when the family was on a vacation. One Sunday father and son went for a hike, during which Theodore Sr. taught Theodore Jr. his very own Sunday School.

  Theodore Sr. taught a Bible class on Sundays. Following his father's example, Theodore Jr. taught his own Bible class for three years as a teenager, before he left for Harvard. He continued the practice during the four years he was in college.

  Theodore Roosevelt Sr. was a wealthy businessman. He worked in the family import business with his own father, who was the first American Roosevelt to become a millionaire. The Quaker ancestors of Theodore Sr.'s mother had come to America with William Penn, the founder of Pennsylvania. She had taught her son that with wealth came an obligation to use that money for some good purpose. Theodore Sr. took her lessons to heart.

Theodore Roosevelt Sr. was a godly, kindhearted man of Christian faith who gave generously of his money and his time. He once said, "I have often thought that unselfishness combined in one word more of the teachings of the Bible than any other in the language."

Theodore Jr. said that his father was "a big, powerful man, with a leonine face, and his heart filled with gentleness for those who needed help or protection."

The elder Roosevelt helped organizations and individuals. He helped to found the Metropolitan Museum of Art and the American Museum of Natural History. He also helped to found the New York City Children's Aid Society and the Newsboys' Lodging House.

Sleeping Quarters at the Newsboys' Lodging House in 1867

In the mid-to-late 1800s, many children in New York City lived in terrible conditions and many worked at odd jobs. One such job was selling newspapers on the street. The Newsboys' Lodging House provided clean housing for five cents a night for newsboys and other needy children. Theodore Roosevelt Sr. visited the children there every Sunday. He learned their names, learned their situations, and gave them advice. From a very early age, he required his children to volunteer there, too. Theodore Sr. also volunteered at a night school for young Italian immigrants.

John Brady was one of the boys the elder Roosevelt got to know at the lodging house. Brady later attended Yale University and Union Seminary. He went into ministry and became a missionary in Alaska. He founded a college for native Alaskans and started a business to make money so that he could help them.

John Brady, Governor of Alaska Territory

President McKinley appointed Brady as territorial governor of Alaska for two terms. When Theodore Roosevelt Jr. became president, he appointed Brady for a third term. Brady was able to meet President Roosevelt while he was in office and express to him his appreciation for his father's help through his ministry at the Newsboys' Lodging House.

## Homeschooling Children with Special Needs

Theodore and Mittie Roosevelt homeschooled children with special needs. Their older daughter Bamie had a form of tuberculosis which caused curvature of the spine. Theodore Sr. was deeply devoted to Bamie and sought out doctors who could help her.

The doctor attending Bamie when she was three fitted her with a restrictive back brace. He instructed Theodore and Mittie to have Bamie spend all day lying face down on a sofa. With heavy hearts, they followed his instruction.

However, when Bamie was four, Theodore found a new doctor for his daughter. Dr. Charles Fayette Taylor believed that physical and mental well-being were closely connected. He fitted Bamie with a new brace and encouraged her to move—not only for her physical well-being, but for her spirits as well.

When Bamie was seven, her father wrote that he was afraid she would have a dreary life and always be in pain. But he made a deliberate effort to brighten her days. On one of his trips to Washington, D.C., during the Civil War, he took Bamie along. She met President Abraham Lincoln and sat on his knee.

Under Dr. Taylor's care, Bamie began to improve. In 1866, when Bamie was eleven years old, Mr. Roosevelt became one of several benefactors who helped to found the New York Orthopedic Dispensary and Hospital to help other children. Dr. Taylor became its head.

Bamie was one of those children who show an early maturity. She was responsible and helpful. Teedie considered her one of the grownups in the family and he and his two younger siblings as the children.

Though never completely cured of her spinal condition, Bamie lived a full life. She married and had a child. She lived in Washington, D.C., while her brother served as president. Roosevelt visited her often and sought her advice.

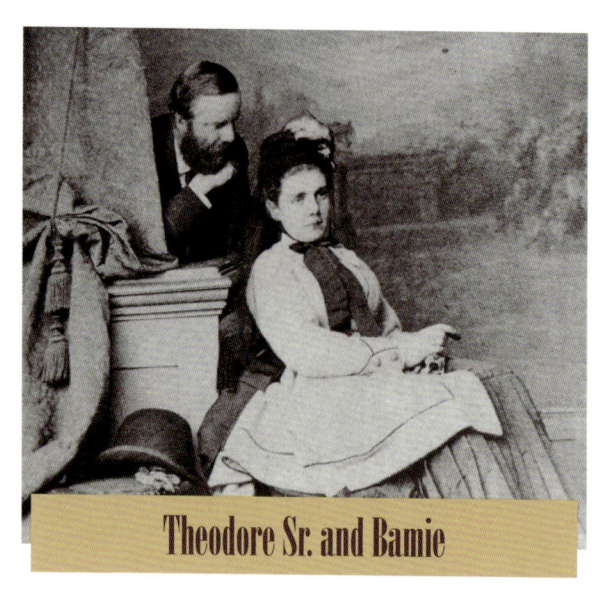

Theodore Sr. and Bamie

The Roosevelts' second child Teedie and their younger daughter Corrine also had special health needs. Both suffered from asthma.

Teedie's case was severe. Again Theodore Sr. devoted himself to the well-being of his child and searched for cures. In his autobiography, President Roosevelt wrote:

> One of my memories is of my father walking up and down the room with me in his arms at night when I was a very small person, and of sitting up in bed gasping, with my father and mother trying to help me.

Sometimes Mr. Roosevelt would take his son into the streets in a carriage, hoping that the cold night air would open his lungs and help him to breathe.

Because of this illness, Teedie had a weak body. His father challenged him to build up his body through exercise and provided exercise equipment for him at home. Teedie used it regularly.

Theodore Jr. was always a weak and sickly child and his severe asthmatic attacks plagued him for many years. However, he had largely overcome these problems by the time he entered Harvard. Theodore Jr. also took up boxing to build up his strength. Many years later, when he became governor of New York, he had a boxing ring installed in the governor's mansion.

Teedie also had poor eyesight, though he did not realize that anything was wrong with his vision until he was twelve years old. His poor eyesight showed up when he could not hit targets well with his gun.

**Theodore Roosevelt Jr., Corinne Roosevelt, Edith Carow, and Elliott Roosevelt in 1875**

    Theodore Jr.'s vision was so bad that when his friends talked about what they read on a billboard, he couldn't even see the letters. He was fitted with glasses and later wrote that the spectacles "literally opened an entirely new world to me." Teedie said, "I never knew how beautiful the world was until I got those spectacles."

# Learning Outdoors and Around the World

Theodore Sr. and Mittie taught their children according to their children's interests. Teedie developed a passion for science. He loved to read about birds and reptiles and to make drawings of them. He found even greater pleasure in collecting specimens of animals for what he called the Roosevelt Museum of Natural History, which he and two of his cousins kept in his family's home.

When Theodore Sr. realized how deeply his son was interested in science, he gave him two books which the future president later passed down to his own children. Theodore Sr. arranged for his son to have lessons in taxidermy. Teedie's teacher had been a colleague of the naturalist and artist John James Audubon.

Teedie Roosevelt's Snowy Owl Specimen

The family's servants and Teedie's siblings sometimes complained about the mess and the smells of his hobby, but Roosevelt later recalled in his autobiography:

> **My father and mother encouraged me warmly in this, as they always did in anything that could give me wholesome pleasure or help to develop me.**

While in his twenties, Theodore Jr. offered his nearly 250 labeled and mounted specimens to the Smithsonian.

Theodore and Mittie believed in giving their children opportunities to be in Creation even in the midst of New York City. They had even removed an exterior wall of a third floor bedroom, turning it into a piazza with a nine-foot railing. The children played on the piazza every day.

The Roosevelts took wonderful field trips and vacations. The family spent every summer in the country, roaming, exploring, riding horses, and climbing trees—a skill their father taught them himself. The children went barefoot much of the time. They watched the haying and harvesting, picked apples, hunted frogs and woodchucks, and gathered nuts to sell to their parents.

In the country, the children had all kinds of pets—cats, dogs, rabbits, a raccoon, and a Shetland pony. Teedie loved these extended vacations so much that he felt eager to go when spring came and sad when the family moved back to town in the late fall.

Theodore and Mittie took their children on two grand tours, one to Europe and one to Egypt, the Holy Land, Syria, Greece, and Constantinople. After the second trip, the Roosevelts arranged for their children to spend the summer with a family in Germany to get an introduction to the German language and to German literature. Teedie thought this family was "the very kindest family imaginable."

**The Roosevelts with Friends in Egypt During the Winter of 1872-1873**

*The Roosevelts traveled in Egypt with the Smith Clift family, also from New York, and some students from Harvard. Here is a group photo from their trip. The Roosevelt children are seated on the floor. From left to right are Anna, Corinne, Theodore, and Elliott.*

# Teedie Grows Up

## Student at Harvard

Theodore Roosevelt Jr.'s education under the direction of his father and mother prepared him well. From the time he was fifteen years old, Teedie studied under a tutor to prepare for entrance exams to Harvard. He later wrote that though he was weak in Latin, Greek, and mathematics, he was strong in science, history, and geography, and was familiar with German and French.

Theodore Jr. entered Harvard just before his 18th birthday in 1876. Soon after he left for school, his father wrote him a letter which included this encouragement: "Take care of your morals first, your health next, and finally your studies."

Theodore Roosevelt Jr. (standing far right) with Harvard Classmates in 1880

Photo at left: Harvard Square in 1874

Years later Theodore Jr. wrote these words to his own son Kermit: "I would rather have a boy of mine stand high in his studies than high in athletics, but I could a great deal rather have him show true manliness of character than show either intellectual or physical prowess."

When Theodore Jr. turned 18 during his first semester at Harvard, he wrote the following in a letter to his mother:

> It seems perfectly wonderful in looking back over my eighteen years of existence, to see how I have literally never spent an unhappy day, unless by my own fault! When I think of this, and also of my intimacy with you all (for I hardly know a boy who is on as intimate and affectionate terms with his family as I am), I feel that I have an immense amount to be thankful for.

In a letter to his father, Theodore Jr. wrote:

> I do not think there is a fellow in college who has a family that love him as much as you all do me, and I am sure that there is no one who has a Father who is also his best and most intimate friend, as you are mine.

During his time at Harvard, Theodore Jr. made two trips to Maine with friends and a local guide named Bill Sewall. Mr. Sewall told his family later that Theodore would take his Bible each day and go alone to a certain place in the woods.

After Roosevelt's death, the Roosevelt Memorial Association placed a plaque at the spot. Known as Bible Point, the location is a Maine State Historic Site.

The plaque reads: "This place, to which a great man in his youth liked to come, to commune with God and with the wonder and beauty of the visible world, is dedicated to the happy memory of Theodore Roosevelt. Stranger, rest here and consider what one man having faith in the right and love for his fellows was able to do for his country."

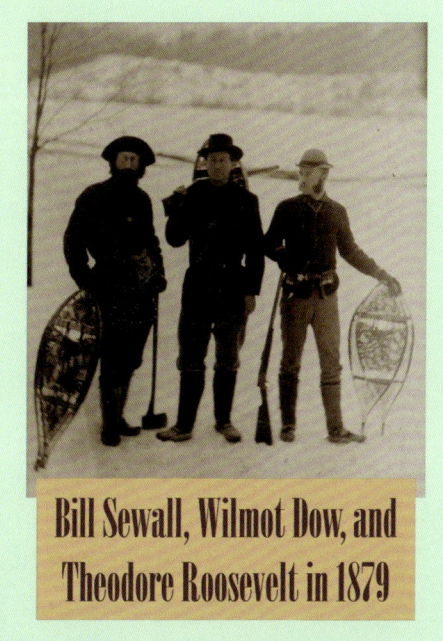

Bill Sewall, Wilmot Dow, and Theodore Roosevelt in 1879

Plaque at Bible Point c. 1921

Theodore Jr. endured a crushing blow during his college years. His father died of cancer in 1878. The elder Roosevelt had kept his illness from his son for several months. When Teedie learned that his father was dying, he rushed home, arriving a few hours too late.

A short time later the broken-hearted son wrote in his journal: "How I wish I could ever do something to keep up his name." Around that same time, he wrote to his mother saying, "I have just been looking over a letter of my dear Father's . . . I do not think I ever could do anything wrong while I have his letters . . . "

His father's ideals were always in Roosevelt's mind. Later in life he said that whenever he faced a difficult decision, he tried to envision what his father would do and then follow through on that course of action to the best of his ability.

Roosevelt appreciated his time at Harvard, but he placed even greater value on the lessons he had learned at home. In his autobiography, Roosevelt recalled:

> **I left college and entered the big world owing more than I can express to the training I had received, especially in my own home; but with much else also to learn if I were to become really fitted to do my part in the world that lay ahead for the generation of Americans to which I belonged.**

Alice Hathaway Lee

## Husband and Father

Theodore Roosevelt fell deeply in love with Alice Hathaway Lee while he was in college. They were married on October 27, 1880, the day Roosevelt turned twenty-two. They visited Europe together the next summer, and Roosevelt was elected to serve in the New York legislature that fall. At the age of twenty-three, he was the youngest person elected to the New York State Assembly.

In 1873 Theodore Sr. had moved his family into a new house in New York City. While Theodore Jr. was serving in the legislature in Albany, his wife Alice lived in that home with his mother and sisters. On February 12, 1884, Alice gave birth there to a daughter, also named Alice.

Tragedy struck the family two days later. Roosevelt hurried home in time to see his Little Motherling before she died of typhoid fever and to hold his wife Alice as she died of undiagnosed kidney failure later that day. Roosevelt left only a brief description of his wife in a private tribute:

> She was beautiful in face and form, and lovelier still in spirit; as a flower she grew, and as a fair young flower she died. Her life had been always in the sunshine; there had never come to her a single great sorrow; and none ever knew her who did not love and revere her for the bright, sunny temper and her saintly unselfishness. Fair, pure, and joyous as a maiden; loving, tender, and happy as a young wife; when she had just become a mother, when her life seemed to be just begun, and when the years seemed so bright before her—then, by a strange and terrible fate, death came to her. And when my heart's dearest died, the light went from my life for ever.

Leaving his daughter Alice in the care of Bamie, the grieving young widower escaped to Dakota Territory, where he became a cattle rancher and a deputy sheriff. Roosevelt chose to deal with his grief by refusing to say his first wife's name again, even to his daughter Alice.

Roosevelt in 1885

Edith Kermit Carow was a longtime friend of the Roosevelt family. After his wife's death, Theodore's friendship with Edith blossomed into romance, and they married on December 2, 1886. Edith welcomed and loved little Alice as her own, and Theodore and Edith had five children together, whom they brought up in a strong, loving, and exciting home.

In 1880, just before his first marriage, Roosevelt had purchased land in the Oyster Bay area of Long Island, where his family had spent summer vacations during his youth. He had planned to build a house there to live with his first wife Alice. After her death, construction proceeded, and Theodore and Edith moved into the house in 1887. They named it Sagamore Hill, and it was their home for the rest of Theodore's life.

### The Roosevelt Family in 1895

*The Roosevelt family sat for this portrait in 1895. From left to right are Theodore, Archie, Ted, Alice, Kermit, Edith, and Ethel. Quentin was born in 1897.*

Sagamore Hill

The Roosevelts at Sagamore Hill c. 1899

# Public Servant and Author

Theodore Roosevelt proved that he learned the lessons his father and mother had taught by word and example. He was an energetic outdoorsman and hunter. He was a public servant, working as a New York police commissioner, assistant secretary of the Navy, a colonel in the Spanish-American War, and governor of New York.

Roosevelt was a prolific writer, publishing three dozen books during his lifetime. His books included biographies, histories, and books about hunting, African animals, and the American West. The former weak and sickly child wrote a book entitled *The Strenuous Life*. The son of a generous philanthropist and Sunday School teacher wrote *Fear God and Take Your Own Part*. The son of Little Motherling wrote *Conservation of Womanhood and Childhood*.

### 1900 Campaign Photo

This campaign photo was composed hastily in 1900. The creator combined an older photo of McKinley from his 1896 campaign with a recent photo of Roosevelt in a similar setting.

# President of the United States

The 1900 Republican convention nominated President William McKinley for a second term of office and nominated Theodore Roosevelt to be his running mate.

Roosevelt campaigned the same way he did almost everything—vigorously! He traveled over 21,000 miles, speaking in 567 cities in 24 states. McKinley and Roosevelt won easily and were inaugurated March 4, 1901.

The following September, the city of Buffalo, New York, hosted a Pan-American Exhibition. This event celebrated the new twentieth century and showcased amazing new technologies, such as uses of electrical power. President McKinley attended the exhibition and gave a speech on September 6.

Later that day, an anti-government assassin shot the president while going through his receiving line. When Secret Service agents wrestled the assassin to the ground, President McKinley said, "Go easy on him, boys." The president also told them to be careful how they told Mrs. McKinley what had happened.

Vice President Roosevelt was on a speaking tour in Vermont that day, but he rushed to Buffalo where he stayed with his close friend, Ansley Wilcox. Doctors believed that McKinley's wounds would heal. When President McKinley's situation improved, they encouraged Vice President Roosevelt to reassure the country by following through with a planned family vacation in the Adirondack Mountains. Roosevelt complied.

Three days later, on September 14, Vice President Roosevelt climbed the highest peak in the Adirondacks.

When he returned from his climb, a messenger brought a telegram telling him that President McKinley was in grave danger. Vice President Roosevelt rode overnight in a hired wagon over rough roads to the nearest train station. At dawn he boarded a special train for Buffalo. When Theodore Roosevelt arrived, President McKinley had been dead for twelve hours, leaving the country without a president.

After paying his respects to Mrs. McKinley, the vice president went again to the Wilcox home. There a federal judge swore in Theodore Roosevelt as the twenty-sixth President of the United States. At forty-two years old, he was the youngest man ever to serve as president.

During the first week of his presidency, President Roosevelt issued his first proclamation, one that mentioned the Christian faith of President McKinley. The proclamation also included the following admonition:

> Now, therefore, I, Theodore Roosevelt, President of the United States of America, do appoint Thursday next, September nineteenth, the day in which the body of the dead President will be laid in its last earthly resting-place, a day of mourning and prayer throughout the United States.
>
> I earnestly recommend all the people to assemble on that day in their respective places of divine

worship, there to bow down in submission to the will of Almighty God and to pay out of full hearts their homage of love and reverence to the great and good President whose death has smitten the nation with bitter grief.

**Booker T. Washington and Theodore Roosevelt**

The month after he became president, Roosevelt caused a stir by inviting his friend Booker T. Washington to dine at the White House. This contemporary print celebrates the event, the first such invitation given by a president to an African American.

**Theodore and Edith Roosevelt in Panama**

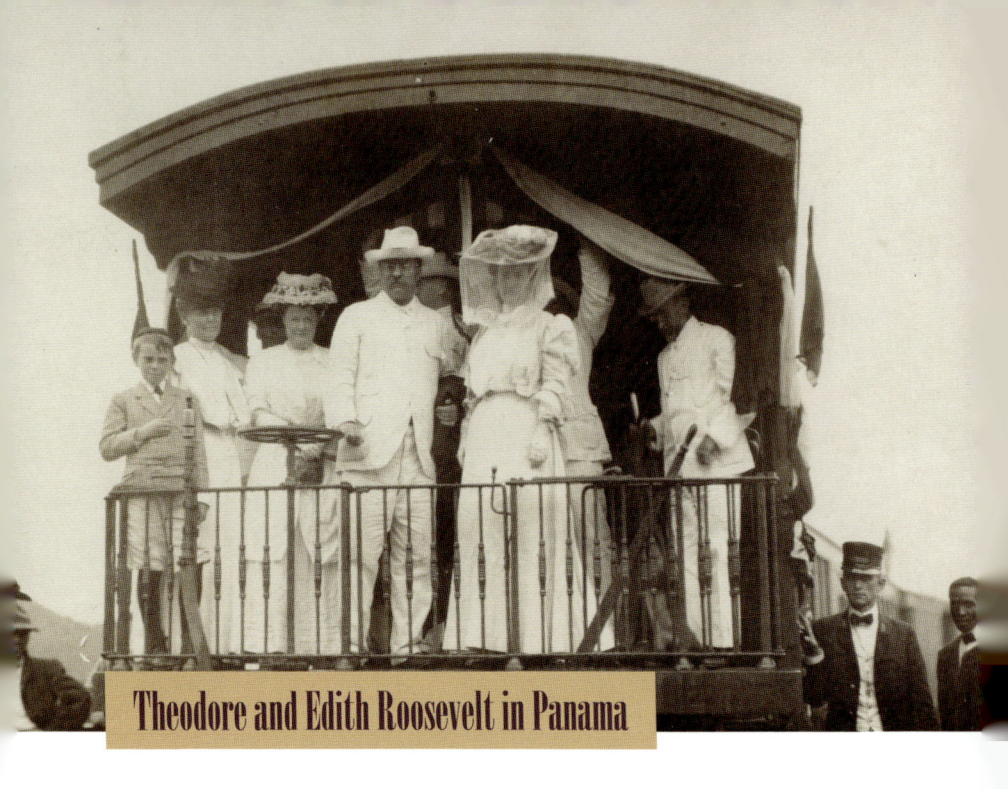

    As president, Theodore Roosevelt supported efforts to make working conditions better for laborers, forced businesses to conduct business with more honesty, supported efforts to make sure America's food was safe, worked to preserve American treasures in national parks, led efforts to build the Panama Canal, and strengthened America's position as a world power. When Roosevelt visited the canal zone in 1906, he became the first United States president to travel outside the country while in office.

    Roosevelt communicated directly to the American people about what government needed to do, calling this role his "bully pulpit." When he spoke in front of crowds, he leaned far forward toward his listeners and spoke with great emotion.

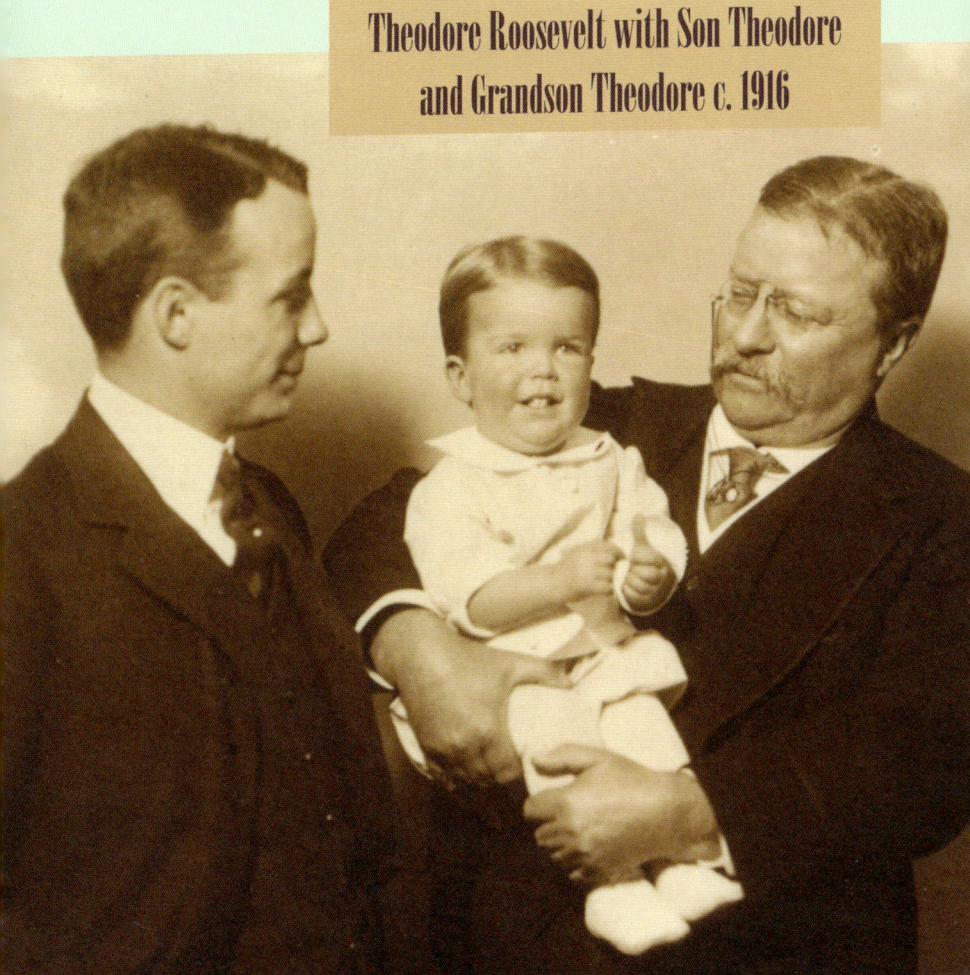

Roosevelt Speaking to a Crowd in 1906

Theodore Roosevelt with Son Theodore and Grandson Theodore c. 1916

In 1904 the American people elected Theodore Roosevelt to a second term. After he left office in 1909, Roosevelt continued to be active on the national scene until his death on January 6, 1919.

The National Association for the Advancement of Colored People (NAACP) was founded in 1909 to end violence and discrimination against minority groups in the United States. Its official magazine was called *The Crisis*. Though Roosevelt's record was not perfect, he had spoken out against injustice and for equality for all Americans. After Roosevelt's death, an editorial in the February 1919 issue of *The Crisis* read, in part:

> The youth of America had no finer inspiration toward which to strive and with the passing of Theodore Roosevelt passes the world's greatest protagonist of lofty ideals and principles. Take him all in all he was a man, generous, impulsive, fearless, loving the public eye, but intent on achieving the public good. And because he was a man so splendidly human even his detractors admired him and his friends could not eulogize him too highly.

*Photo at right: Elliott (left) and Theodore Roosevelt in 1880*

# What We Can Learn

Homeschooling was a wonderful foundation and launching pad for each of Theodore and Mittie Roosevelt's children. But homeschooling was not a guarantee of a wonderful future. Each of the children had to choose what he or she would do with that foundation. Our holy and perfect Father God has children who choose to reject his training. This can also happen in homeschooling families.

Theodore Roosevelt's younger brother Elliott was homeschooled along with the rest of his siblings. But as a young man Elliott chose to abuse alcohol. He was later unfaithful to his wife. His daughter Eleanor, who went on to marry her distant cousin Franklin Delano Roosevelt, grew up without her father. Elliott died unhappy and alone at age thirty-four.

For all his virtues, President Theodore Roosevelt was not perfect. He made some choices and held some views that seem out-of-step with the principles given to us in the Bible. However, President Roosevelt followed the example of his parents and made conscious choices to do great good in his family and his country.

You can homeschool like Theodore and Mittie Roosevelt. You and your children—and perhaps your country and even the world—will be glad you did. Turn the page for practical ideas to get you started right away.

# You Can Homeschool Like Theodore and Mittie

**Love** your children deeply and try in every way you can imagine to show them your love is true.

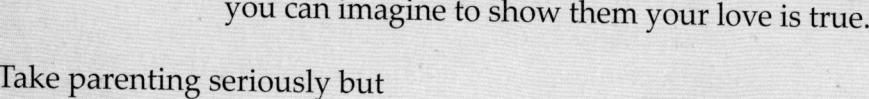

Take parenting seriously but **have a blast** while you do.

Find out what **fascinates** your children and give them opportunities to explore those interests.

Take your children to **wonderful places**, even if they are only a few minutes or hours away.

Teach your children to **serve** others.

Provide lots of great books and **time** in your children's schedule to read them.

Spend time in **God's Creation**.

Give your children the opportunity to spend the bulk of their time with their very own **family**: mama and daddy and brothers and sisters and extended family.

Learn to **get along** with your husband or wife, despite your differences, even if other people are going to war over those very same differences.

Find ways to help your children with their **special needs**—physical, mental, or emotional.

Teach your children's hearts and souls, as well as their minds, and pay close attention to their **character**.

Live lives of joy and service and purpose and **faith** that your children can emulate.

*Birds Theodore Jr. collected in Egypt*

# Roosevelt Historical Sites

You can learn more about the Roosevelts at these historical sites and parks around the country.

**Theodore Roosevelt Island**
Washington, DC
BestTrips.guide/trid67

**Bulloch Hall**
Roswell, GA
BestTrips.guide/bhga34

**Bible Point State Historic Site**
Island Falls, ME
BestTrips.guide/bpsh79

**Theodore Roosevelt Collection and Gallery at Harvard Library**
Cambridge, MA
BestTrips.guide/trma76

**Theodore Roosevelt Inaugural National Historic Site**
Buffalo, NY
BestTrips.guide/trin01

**Theodore Roosevelt Birthplace National Historic Site**
New York, NY
BestTrips.guide/trbh48

**Theodore Roosevelt Memorial**
New York, NY
BestTrips.guide/trmn77

**Sagamore Hill National Historic Site**
Oyster Bay, NY
BestTrips.guide/shnh85

**Theodore Roosevelt Gravesite**
Oyster Bay, NY
BestTrips.guide/trgn19

**Theodore Roosevelt National Park**
North Dakota
BestTrips.guide/trnp83

**Pine Knot**
Keene, VA
BestTrips.guide/pkva05

## Sources

McCullough, David. *Mornings on Horseback.* New York: Simon & Schuster, 2001.
National Park Service
Roosevelt, Theodore. *Theodore Roosevelt: An Autobiography.* New York: Charles Scribner's Sons, 1920.
Theodore Roosevelt Collection, Houghton Library, Harvard University